P9-AOM-080

Protecting Habitats

PROTECTING
Mountain
Habitats

Clifton Park - Halfmoon Public Library
475 Moe Road
Clifton Park, New York 12065

Robert Snedden

GARETH**STEVENS**
GS
P U B L I S H I N G
A Member of the WRC Media Family of Companies

Please visit our web site at: www.garethstevens.com
For a free color catalog describing Gareth Stevens Publishing's list of high-quality books
and multimedia programs, call 1-800-542-2595 (USA) or 1-800-387-3178 (Canada).
Gareth Stevens Publishing's fax: (414) 332-3567

Library of Congress Cataloging-in-Publication Data

Snedden, Robert.
    Protecting mountain habitats / Robert Snedden. — North American ed.
    p. cm. — (Protecting habitats)
    Includes index.
    ISBN 0-8368-4991-4 (lib. bdg.)
    1. Mountains—Juvenile literature. 2. Habitat conservation—Juvenile literature.
  I. Title. II. Series.
  QH87.S635   2005
  577.5'3—dc22   2005042626

This North American edition first published in 2006 by
Gareth Stevens Publishing
A Member of the WRC Media Family of Companies
330 West Olive Street, Suite 100
Milwaukee, WI 53212 USA

Designer: Rita Storey
Editor: Sarah Ridley
Art Director: Jonathan Hair
Editor-in-Chief: John C. Miles
Picture Research: Susan Mennell
Map and graph artwork: Ian Thompson

Gareth Stevens Editor: Gini Holland
Gareth Stevens Cover Design: Dave Kowalski

Photo credits: Ecoscene: cover, 1, 4 (Anthony Cooper), 9 (Robert Weight), 12 (Promeck Services), 13 (Paul
Thompson), 22 (Sally Morgan), 24 (Fritz Polking); Oxford Scientific Films: 16 (Mark Jones), 23 (Mary Plage),
26 (Stephen Miller); Photolibrary.com: 21; Still Pictures: 5, 8 (Jeremy Woodhouse), 11 (Markus Dlouhy), 14 (M.
& C. Denis-Huot), 17 (M. Boulton), 19 (Joerg Boethling), 20 (Knut Mueller), 25 (F. Suchel)

Printed in the United States of America

1 2 3 4 5 6 7 8 9 09 08 07 06 05

CONTENTS

All about Mountains

Mountains have always fascinated people. Their remoteness and beauty are inspiring. Until adventurers and explorers went up to take a look, many people believed that mountains were the home of the gods.

Today, mountains are under threat. Ski lifts scar the mountainsides. Farmers drive their herds high into the alpine meadows to graze, eroding the soil and threatening the fragile ecosystem. Less visible, but no less serious, global warming pushes mountain plants and animals toward extinction as they struggle to escape its effects.

Shaping the World

Mountains shape the land around them in many ways. They affect the weather, blocking rainfall so that the land in the

The Rocky Mountains, shown here in winter at Banff, Alberta, Canada, are challenging to climb.

4

ISLAND REFUGES

A mountain stands out in the landscape like an island in the middle of an ocean. These are places where animals, as well as humans, have found refuge from the pressures of living in the lowlands. Species driven out by human activity in the lowlands may survive here. Mountains have been described as "islands of biodiversity" because there is a huge variety of plants and animals living there that are quite different from those found in the surrounding lowlands. In the mountains, there are living things found nowhere else in the world.

shadow of a mountain range can become a parched desert. Mountains can also give water to the land, as the melting snow and ice from their peaks run down to feed rivers that lead from mountain ranges to the sea.

Mountains have also played their part in shaping history. Their huge size and sheer slopes formed impassable barriers to all but the most determined invaders and explorers. Many mountain ranges continue to mark the geographical boundaries between one country and another. A town or village in the mountains has ready-made natural defenses, and for centuries the very remoteness of mountains has made them places of refuge for people fleeing from persecution elsewhere.

Today, aircraft fly over mountain ranges, and road and railway links tunnel through them. Although people can now cross mountains, they remain extraordinary features of our landscape.

The mighty Andes mountains run the length of South America. Here, vicuña graze near salt pans in the Altiplano region of Chile.

Where to Find Mountains

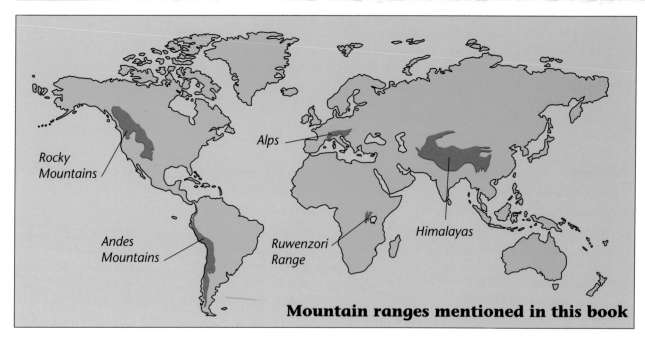

Rocky Mountains

Alps

Andes Mountains

Ruwenzori Range

Himalayas

Mountain ranges mentioned in this book

Mountains exist in every continent in the world. They cover about a fifth of the Earth's land surface and there are many more hidden from sight beneath the ocean. Most mountains lie in groups called ranges, each with their own characteristic plants and wildlife.

The Himalayas

Himalaya means "house of the snow." More than twenty of the world's tallest mountains are in this range, including Mount Everest, at 29,020 feet (8,848 meters). The Himalayan mountain chain stretches for 1,500 miles (2,400 kilometers), crossing the countries of Bhutan, Nepal, Tibet, India, and Pakistan.

On the lower Himalayan slopes — up to about 6,600 feet (2,000 meters) or so above sea level — chestnut trees, laurels, and oaks grow. Tea plants and rhododendron bushes are also common. Pine trees and other conifers grow on the higher slopes up to about 11,500 feet (3,500 m).

In the southern Himalayas, the lower slopes support tropical forest, which contains tigers, monkeys, and Asian elephants. Higher up live animals such as the yak.

The Rocky Mountains

The Rocky Mountains run like a backbone down about 3,000 miles (4,800 km) of North America, from northern Alberta, Canada, down to New Mexico in the south. The tallest peak in the Rockies is Mount Elbert in Colorado. The Missouri, Columbia, and Rio Grande rivers all begin in the Rockies. Because the Rockies run so far from north to south, they stretch across a number of climate zones and are home to a wide range of plants and animals.

The Andes

The Andes mountain range is the longest in the world and also has some of the highest

The surface of our planet is never still. The seemingly solid crust of the Earth is made up of enormous, slow-moving segments called plates. Where two plates collide, they buckle up, forming huge mountain ranges. Mountain ranges do not grow quickly. The Himalayas, for example, were born when the plate carrying India collided with the plate carrying part of Asia (*see diagram at right*). Fifty million years later, the mountains of the Himalayas are still growing by about half an inch (1 cm) every year.

Mountains can also be formed when molten rock beneath Earth's surface forces its way up through a weakness in the crust, forming a volcano. The tallest mountain in Africa, Kilimanjaro, is a volcano, and so too is the world's tallest mountain, Mauna Kea, in the Hawaiian Islands. Mauna Kea is more than 32,800 feet (10,000 m) tall, but the lower 19,680 feet (6,000 m) hide beneath the Pacific Ocean.

This diagram shows the stages by which the Indian plate collided with the Asian plate millions of years ago, creating the Himalayas.

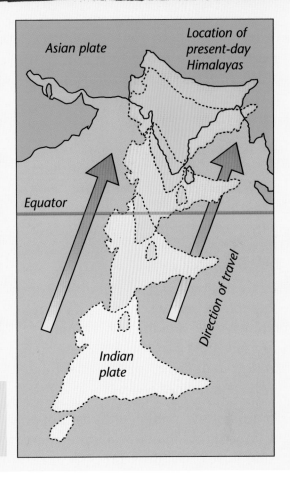

Asian plate

Location of present-day Himalayas

Equator

Direction of travel

Indian plate

mountains, with Mount Aconcagua, at 22,830 feet (6,960 m), the tallest in the range. The Andes run for more than 4,500 miles (7,200 km) along the western edge of South America from Panama to Cape Horn at the tip of Chile. Like the Rockies, the Andes span a range of climates.

The Ruwenzori Range

The small Ruwenzori range is located in eastern Africa, on the border that runs between Uganda and the Democratic Republic of Congo. It is about 75 miles (120 km) long and 40 miles (65 km) wide. The highest peak in the range soars to 16,761 feet (5,109 m) and is permanently snowcapped. Along with the isolated Mount Kilimanjaro and Mount Kenya, these are the only snowcapped mountains in Africa.

The Alps

The Alps are the largest mountain range in Europe, stretching in a 620-mile (1,000-km) curve from southern Germany and Austria down through Switzerland, southern France, and northern Italy almost to the Mediterranean Sea. The highest peak, Mont Blanc, lies between France, Italy, and Switzerland and is more than 15,750 feet (4,800 m) high. The name Alps comes from Latin and means "high mountains," so high-altitude habitats around the world are referred to as "alpine" habitats.

Mountain Science

Conditions on a mountain can change rapidly, making it a challenging environment for the plants and animals that live there.

Take a Deep Breath

If you climb high into hills or mountains, or go skiing, it might not be simply lack of fitness that makes you breathe more heavily. One very important factor that mountain climbers have to consider is that the higher you climb, the thinner the air becomes and the less essential oxygen there is available to breathe. Most of the climbers who have made it to the top of Mount Everest have taken oxygen cylinders and breathing equipment with them, although a few have managed without.

Animals that live at high altitudes not only have larger lungs than low-altitude animals but also have about three times as many of the red blood cells that are responsible for carrying oxygen from the lungs to the rest of the body. People who live at high altitudes, such as the Sherpas of the Himalayas and the people of the Andes, are similarly adapted. Animals that move up and down the slopes over the course of the year make adjustments to their red-blood cell count, making more red blood cells as they move back to higher altitudes. Human mountain climbers and competitive skiers can also become acclimatized to high altitudes in this way.

Temperature Drop

Not only does the air get thinner at high altitudes, but the temperature also drops. For every 330 feet (100 m) climbed, the temperature will drop by between 1° and 2° Fahrenheit (0.6° and 1°C), depending on how dry the air is. It is these low temperatures that explain why mountain peaks are often covered in snow.

The atmosphere becomes much thinner and colder at high altitudes. This photograph shows part of Grand Teton National Park in Wyoming.

Above a certain point, called the snow line, the temperature falls below freezing. The height of the snow line will depend on where in the world the mountain is situated. A mountain in the tropics, where the surrounding climate is warm, will have a high snow line, perhaps more than 13,000 feet (4,000 m) up. A mountain in the polar regions, with low temperatures all year long, will be almost entirely snow-covered. High winds at the top of a mountain can make it feel extremely cold.

Conditions on a mountain in the tropics can be rather odd. High up on the mountain, the air is clear but thin, so the sun can warm the ground very quickly. Thin air, however, is not good at trapping heat, and as soon as the sun disappears, the temperature plummets again.

RADIATION HAZARD

Another high-altitude hazard comes from ultraviolet (UV) radiation from the sun. At lower levels, the atmosphere blocks out much of this harmful radiation, although enough gets through to damage unprotected skin in the summer. In response, mountain animals are often dark in color, as their black pigment shields them from harmful UV rays and helps prevent damage to the animal. UV rays are also very harmful to the eyes, which is one of the reasons that mountaineers, such as the one shown below, wear protective goggles.

Water and Weather

The influence of mountains on the areas around them is huge. Half the people in the world rely on rivers fed by mountain streams. Mountains store water in the form of snow and ice that thaws and feeds the rivers in spring. Mountains also have a big effect on the weather patterns of lower-lying areas.

World Water Towers

Snow falling on mountaintops does not melt because it is so cold there. Year after year, snow builds up, and the weight compresses the lower layers into ice, forming a glacier. A glacier is like a giant river of ice that flows slowly down the mountainside. Eventually, the lower tongue of the glacier moves down past the snow line, where the temperature rises above freezing. Here, it begins to melt, creating streams that feed into rivers, bringing vital fresh water to the lowlands surrounding the mountain range. Because mountain streams are fed from the frozen glacier reservoirs, rivers with their sources in high mountain ranges continue to flow, even in times of drought.

Weather Patterns

Airflow hitting a mountain is forced upward. As it rises, the air cools, and any moisture carried in it will condense and fall as rain or snow. The land on the windward side of the mountain benefits from this rainfall, and the slopes on this side may be densely forested. On the other side of the mountain, however, things may be quite different. By the time the clouds have moved over the mountain, they have much less moisture in them. Additionally, as the air moves down the mountain it warms up. Warm air can carry more moisture, so its moisture is less likely to fall as rain.

The land on the dry side of the mountain is said to be in a rain shadow. The Andes mountain range shelters the Atacama Desert so well that in some places it hasn't rained for hundreds of years. The grassy steppes of northern Asia are kept dry by the Urals to the west and the Altai mountains to the south. The mountains are also why Siberian winters are so cold: They trap freezing air flowing in from the Arctic.

THE WIND FROM THE MOUNTAINS

The cold, dense air at the top of a mountain does not just sit there. Gravity pulls it back down the mountain, blowing it into the lowlands as wind. Mountain valleys and gullies can channel and focus the wind, causing it to blow harder.

One such wind is the mistral, which blows down from the Alps, across southern France and the Mediterranean at speeds that can reach about 60 miles per hour (100 km/h).

Another mountain wind is the chinook, or Snow Eater, of North America. As the air sinks down from the Rocky Mountains, it is compressed and gets warmer. Often following an intensely cold spell, the chinook can cause rapid local warming and snow melt.

Melting ice and snow can produce spectacular mountain waterfalls, such as this one in Iceland.

Mountain Zones

From the heat of the tropics around the equator to the frozen wastelands of the polar regions in the far north and south, the world is divided into a number of climate zones. Going up a mountain is a little like traveling through a series of changing climate zones piled one above another within the space of a few hundred yards.

The Zones

Just like world climate zones, mountain zones are divided according to the type of plants that live there. These plants have adapted to the changing conditions found at increasing altitudes. Climbers ascend through a number of different biomes, meaning continuous stretches of similar natural habitat. Moving through broad-leaved forest at the bottom of the mountain, climbers pass into evergreen forest, grassland, and tundra to reach the alpine biome just beneath the snow line. Higher than this, on the mountain equivalent of the polar ice caps, very little can survive on the bare rocks and snowfields of the high peaks.

A mountain in a temperate climate zone will have warm summers and cool winters, similar to those in the surrounding landscape. These conditions suit broad-leaved trees that shed their leaves in the winter, and the lower slopes of a mountain may be thickly forested.

Meadows on the upper slopes of mountain ranges are filled with flowers in summer. Here, globe buttercups flourish in the Alps.

SPECIAL CONDITIONS

As you travel north or south from the equator in wintertime, the length of the days gets shorter. From top to bottom of a mountain, however, the length of day is just the same, which creates some interesting conditions for plants living in mountain habitats. At the top of a mountain it is cold all the time, but the plants living there get as much sunlight as those on the lowest slopes. Therefore, mountaintop plants are quite unlike those of, for example, the Arctic, which have had to adapt to both cold and lack of light in winter.

Needle-bearing trees called conifers are adapted to survive in snowy conditions, as shown in this photograph taken near Soll in Austria.

Farther up the mountain. conditions are cooler. Broad-leaved trees like the oak cannot survive here. Conifers, trees that are better suited to low temperatures, become more numerous on the higher slopes, just as they are in the northern forests.

The Tree Line

Even the well-adapted conifers cannot survive all the way up the mountainside. Above a certain height, conditions become so harsh that no trees can grow. This height is called the tree line. Above the tree line, there are other, smaller plants. This zone is called the alpine meadow, and in spring it can be covered in a dazzling display of wild flowers.

Higher than the alpine meadows on the highest mountains, tough lichens manage to cling to bare rocks (*see page 15*). Higher still, above the snow line, no plants can live in the frozen ice fields. Some tough survivors, however, still manage to live here: Just under the surface of the snow, millions of microscopic single-celled algae thrive.

13

Mountain Plants

Some mountain plants appear strange but are adapted to survive in highland conditions. This giant senecon is from the Ruwenzori Range in Africa.

Mountain plants have developed different ways of surviving according to how high up the mountain they live. At the foot of the mountain, vegetation — such as dense, broad-leaved forest — will be much the same as it is in surrounding lowland areas. As you ascend the slopes, broad-leaved trees give way to plants better adapted to living at higher altitudes.

Mountain Conifers

Conifers have dark green leaves that they keep throughout the year. Dark leaves absorb heat from the sun more quickly than light-colored leaves do, and warm leaves make food faster than cold ones. By keeping its leaves all year long, the tree is ready to make food and to do so efficiently whenever the sun appears. Its cone shape is another way the conifer adapts to life at high altitudes. As the temperature falls higher up the mountain, there is a greater likelihood of snow falling. Because of the tree's shape, most snow that settles on the conifer will slide off without damaging its branches. Conifers also have shallow root systems that spread out widely in thin soil.

Alpine Meadows

Alpine plants are brightly colored to attract the few insect pollinators that live there. At still higher altitudes, the soil cover becomes even thinner and the bare rock of the mountaintop is exposed. A few species of plants are able to take root in little pockets of soil trapped between the rocks. These high-altitude plants often have dark leaves in order to absorb as much heat as possible from the sun and hairy surfaces that act as a blanket, holding on to the little warmth that is available. Alpine plants are much smaller than plants at lower altitudes. Tall plants would be torn apart by the winds.

High-Altitude Team

The only plants that grow on the bare mountain rocks are lichens. Lichens are extremely slow-growing, spreading only a few inches over decades. A lichen isn't a flowering plant. It is actually a partnership between simple plants called algae and fungi. The fungus grips the rock surface, producing chemicals that dissolve the rock as it clings, and the alga makes food from sunlight for both to share. It takes teamwork to survive in the high mountains.

ONE POTATO, TWO POTATO

About twenty plant varieties supply 80 percent of the food eaten by the human race. Six of them — maize, barley, sorghum, apples, tomatoes, and potatoes — were first discovered in mountain areas. The Andes are the home of the potato, one of the world's most important vegetable crops. The wild potato was discovered growing in the mountains by people living in what is now the country of Peru, and it was first grown as a crop about 4,500 years ago. Andean farmers know of more than two hundred varieties of potato growing in the mountains. Wild potatoes will grow where the climate is too cold for other staple crops, such as wheat or corn.

Mountain Animals

Mountainous regions are difficult places in which to survive, and animals living there face a range of weather conditions. In fact, the highest mountain environment is similar in some ways to that of the Earth's polar regions, although obviously there are differences. One big difference, mentioned earlier, is that the air grows thinner at high altitude; mountain animals have adapted to make maximum use of the oxygen that is available.

Keeping Warm

Another obvious problem faced by all mountain animals is the cold. Only warm-blooded animals can survive in the highest reaches of the mountains. Although some reptiles and amphibians are found as high up as the coniferous forests, there are none in the high mountain regions above the tree line. These cold-blooded creatures rely on the warmth of the sun, and there just is not enough warmth for them to survive up there. They also lack anything in the way of insulating fur or feathers.

HIGH-FLYING BIRDS

Several types of birds are found in mountains, including some of the most spectacular in the world. The Andes, for example, are home to both the mighty Andean condor, one of the world's biggest and rarest birds of prey, and the world's highest altitude hummingbirds, such as the Estella hummingbird, which can be found living nearly 16,400 feet (5,000 m) up.

Hikers in the mountains of Canada often find their campsites being visited by birds called whiskey-jacks. These bold jays will quickly snatch away any unattended morsels of food.

The Andean condor's huge wings are adapted for riding the warm air currents found in the Andes.

The wild yak's thick, hairy coat protects it from the biting Himalayan winds.

Alpine animals have adapted to the cold in a number of ways. Some, such as the black bears of the Rocky Mountain forests, escape the worst of the winter cold by going into hibernation in a warm, secure den until conditions improve in the spring. Other animals leave the higher parts of the mountain and migrate down to the lower, warmer slopes as winter approaches. When spring returns, these animals climb back up.

Animals such as mountain goats follow the snow line as it moves up and down the mountain with the changing seasons. As the retreating snow exposes the soil, the goats dig up the roots and bulbs of alpine plants. The yak is the highest-altitude mountain mammal; it manages to feed on lichens scraped from rocks that rest about 20,000 feet (6,000 m) up in the Himalayas.

Most mountain mammals are protected from the cold by thick, furry coats and layers of insulating fat. The body shape of a mountain animal may be different from that of its lowland relatives. Its legs, tail, and ears are likely to be shorter — all adaptations to reduce the loss of heat.

Get a Grip!

Mountain animals have to be agile and well-balanced enough to make their way across difficult terrain without falling or slipping down the mountain. The Himalayan yak, for example, has short legs and broad hooves with large dewclaws on the inside leg that help it grip the often treacherous surfaces of its mountain habitat. The Rocky Mountain bighorn sheep keeps a sure-footed grip on steep mountain slopes with its soft and flexible hooves.

Mountain People

Mountains are challenging environments for people to live in, but although it is tough to make a living in the mountains, many people around the world still manage to do so. About one tenth of the world's population — roughly 600 million people — live in mountainous regions. Half of them live in the Himalayas, the Andes, and the mountain ranges of Africa.

Survival Skills

Mountain people often live in conditions that would seem harsh to most of us. In developing countries in particular, many mountain people live as nomads, hunters and gatherers, traders, small farmers, and herders. Because their lives depend on being knowledgeable about their environment, mountain people have built up a wealth of experience with the mountains and their plants and animals. Scientists now realize that the knowledge of mountain people can help protect the fragile mountain environment (*see pages 25–27*).

Sherpas

Among the most famous of the mountain peoples are the Sherpas of the Himalayas. Around 35,000 to 40,000 Sherpas live in the mountains of Nepal and some also live in India, Bhutan, and Tibet. For centuries, the Sherpas have lived here as farmers, yak herders, and traders. These tough, resourceful people have a phenomenal reputation as climbers. In 1953, Tenzing Norgay Sherpa, along with New Zealander Sir Edmund Hillary, became the first men to reach the summit of Mount Everest. Today, a significant number of Sherpas earn their living from guiding climbers in the Himalayas (*see page 20*). Some people are concerned that the lifestyle of the Sherpas is being changed and Westernized by their increasing dependence on tourist money.

People of the Altiplano

The Altiplano, or high plains, lie between the forests of the Amazon and the peaks of the Andes. This harsh environment of poor soils, wide variations in temperature, and little plant or animal life lies at an average

WORKING IN HARMONY

Mountain valleys often have fine fertile soils and may also be sheltered and warm. If it were not for the steep slopes, they would be ideal for farming. To adapt to these conditions people in many parts of the world, particularly in Southeast Asia, have shaped the lower mountain slopes into a series of flat terraces that run around the hillside. Important food crops, such as rice, have been produced in terraced farms for many centuries. Terracing is a good example of people working in harmony with the mountain environment. The terraces are walled to keep in water and prevent the soil from being washed downhill. Other forms of agriculture, in which the ground is simply plowed up or grazed by animals, may cause erosion, as the soil is loosened and washes away, with consequent habitat loss.

height of 13,000 feet (4,000 m) above sea level. Despite this height, it is here that the peoples of the Andes, mainly Aymara and Quechua Indians, make their living. The Andean people have become adapted to high-altitude life. Their hearts and lungs are bigger than those of most lowlanders, helping them to cope with the lack of oxygen. An important crop here is the potato, some varieties of which can be grown as high up as 15,000 feet (4,500 m). Herds of alpaca and llamas are also kept, feeding on the tough grasses that grow as high as the so-called frost deserts at 16,500 feet (5,000 m).

Two traditionally dressed Sherpa women from the Himalayas spin yarn from plant fibers.

Mountains in Danger

Mountains look solid and unchanging, and mountain habitats can seem remote and safe from human interference. Sadly, they are not. Threats to the mountain environment are increasing yearly.

Population Pressure

Farmers in many parts of the world find themselves under increasing pressure to find more land on which to grow crops to feed a growing, hungry population. The mountain habitats of Africa, in particular, are being hard hit. Almost half the mountain regions of Africa are now farmed in some way, with a third of the mountain habitat being grazed by animals. The pressure of the animals' hooves breaks up the fragile mountain soil, causing erosion. At the same time, the animals consume the very plants that help hold the soil together.

The Tourist Toll

For many people of the world's wealthier nations, the mountains have become a kind of playground. Modern means of transportation are making remote regions accessible to anyone who can afford to go there. Around seventy million people around the world enjoy winter sports, but they can put pressure on fragile mountain environments.

In 1964, twenty trekkers from other parts of the world arrived in the Everest region of Nepal. By 2000, trekker tourist numbers had increased to twenty-seven thousand. Four-fifths of the households in the region now get a major part of their income from tourism. The number of trekkers is taking a toll on the mountain environment. It is estimated that about seventeen tons of trash left behind by trekkers are strewn along every mile of the Everest trail.

Many African mountain regions have been cleared for farming and grazing.

Tourists bring money with them, and that money attracts people eager to offer the services for which tourists will pay. In the Alps, for example, many families are moving from small farming communities to live and work around a handful of large tourist resorts. This trend can cause an increase in soil erosion in the abandoned farming areas. Traditional farming methods help anchor the soil and keep it healthy. When the farmers depart, the untended soil is exposed to the full harshness of the mountain climate and erodes away.

Downhill Disasters Loom

The popularity of skiing vacations, particularly in the mountains of Europe and North America, puts huge pressure on the mountain environment. This pressure comes not only from building chalets, ski lifts, and cable cars that scar the hillsides, but also from the pollution from the exhausts of the countless vehicles ferrying skiers and their equipment up and down the mountainside. The use of off-road vehicles and snowmobiles also causes damage to the slopes. Snow sports threaten the ecology of the very mountains on which these sports depend. Global warming, however, may be a bigger threat, closing ski resorts altogether.

The popularity of ski resorts and tourism has put enormous pressure on fragile mountain habitats.

Mountains and Climate Change

World temperatures are rising. Some insist this trend is due to normal variations in world climate. Others cite evidence to show that the main cause of global warming is increased worldwide human use of fossil fuels such as oil — especially as gasoline — and coal. Burning fossil fuels releases carbon dioxide into the atmosphere. Increased levels of carbon dioxide act like a greenhouse, preventing heat from escaping into space. Mountain habitats and the plants and animals that live there are seen as particularly vulnerable to this warming effect.

Moving Mountain Zones

The rise in global temperatures is now being felt all through the mountain habitat zones. According to some researchers, a rise of three degrees or so in the world's temperature will shift the mountain climate zones up by about 1,640 feet (500 m). No one can be quite sure what effect long-term global warming might have on mountain habitats, but already some changes can be observed. A study in Norway found that many plants have moved up to 980 feet (300 m) higher in the last sixty years. For those plants and animals at the top of the mountain ranges, there just will not be anywhere left to go.

Global warming may be causing glaciers, such as this one in Alberta, Canada, to melt.

The loss of snow cover on the mountains would have a catastrophic effect on those mountain communities that depend on skiing and other winter sports for their income. As global warming pushes the snow line ever higher, many ski resorts will find themselves without any reliable snowfall. Avalanches from above would be hazardous for skiers.

If the snowfields vanish, all that would be left would be bare rock with no soil where the alpine meadow plants could colonize. Meanwhile, the expanding conifer forests would threaten these alpine meadow plants from below as the upper limit of the tree line grew higher. At the same time, of course, the broad-leaf forest would be pushing from below into the conifers. All layers of the mountain habitat would push upward, destroying vulnerable mountain life.

Some of the world's rarest wildlife is at severe risk. Animals such as the Tibetan yak are so well adapted to cold conditions that they would find it hard to survive if their homes disappear. In Australia, the mountain pygmy possum is likely to become extinct if average temperatures rise a single degree.

Shrinking Glaciers

In practically every mountain range in the world, from Greenland to the Rockies and from the Alps to the Andes, ice fields and glaciers are shrinking at an alarming rate. Glaciers in the Alps are only half as big as they were a century ago. If current trends continue, by the end of this century Glacier National Park, set in the northern Rocky Mountains, will have to be renamed — there will not be any glaciers left.

The disappearance of glaciers will have a huge effect. Exposed mountaintops will erode, increasing rock slides and avalanches that will damage lower slopes. Mountain streams and rivers, fed by the glaciers, will first flood with melting ice and snow and then gradually begin to dry up.

The yak is one of many mountain animals that are under threat worldwide.

Saving Mountain Wildlife

Mountain wildlife is hardy and well-adjusted to its often harsh habitat. The plants and animals of the mountains are in balance with their habitat. If their habitat is damaged, however, that balance is lost.

Year of the Mountains

Mountains were once seen as environmental "poor relations" compared to the oceans and the rain forests. There was plenty of publicity for saving rain forest animals and whales and dolphins, but not much for the

One of the most severely endangered animals in the world is the mountain gorilla, which lives in the mist-covered highlands of Central Africa.

PROTECTED MOUNTAINS

Many mountain areas around the world are protected by law as nature reserves or national parks. North East Greenland National Park (*below*), established in 1974, is the largest protected area in the world and covers an area larger than Britain and France put together. Even so, less than one tenth of the world's mountain habitats enjoy any sort of protection.

alpine meadows. In fact, although rain forest destruction is widely condemned, the forests that are disappearing most quickly are the cloud forests of the Andes and of the tropical mountains of Africa and Southeast Asia.

In 2002, an attempt was made to change that when the International Year of Mountains was celebrated. By July 2004, forty countries, from Afghanistan to Venezuela, and organizations such as the World Bank, UNESCO, and the World Wildlife Fund had joined together to form the Mountain Partnership. Their goal is to protect mountain habitats and improve the lives of mountain people.

Local Skills

Mountain people know better than anyone what treasures are being lost when their fragile mountain environment is damaged. A few years ago, in the Indian Himalayas, national foresters listed twenty-five different types of plants that had been destroyed by logging and mining operations in the area. In contrast, local mountain women could actually identify 145 types of plants lost to the miners and loggers.

In most cases, mountain people do not own the land they live on. Laws that give mountain communities the right to decide what happens to their homes would be a big step forward in helping to preserve the mountain environment. Mountain people know, for example, that in a habitat as varied as the mountains, traditional sheep and goat farming and small-scale agriculture work best. In the mountains of Nepal, for instance, two thousand varieties of rice are grown. Replacing this traditionally diverse approach by plowing up the land, introducing single-crop cultivation, or driving herds of cows up onto the alpine meadows, could be disastrous.

Collecting Knowledge

Perhaps because they are often inaccessible and difficult to live in, mountains are one of the least studied natural habitats. If we are to preserve the variety of mountain habitats in the world, however, we have to begin to understand how they work. Clearly, the native peoples of the mountains have a great storehouse of knowledge that we can draw on. We can also use modern advances in technology, such as radio tracking devices, to monitor the movements of animals across the mountains and record their numbers.

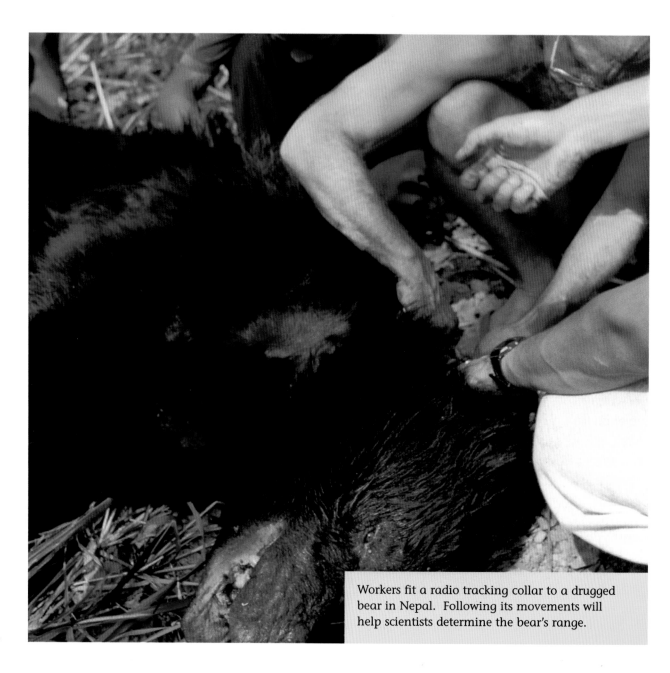

Workers fit a radio tracking collar to a drugged bear in Nepal. Following its movements will help scientists determine the bear's range.

MOUNTAIN WOMEN

"If you want to know, ask the women." Researchers studying mountain farming techniques often find themselves directed to women if they have questions about seeds and plants. It is the women of the mountain peoples who hold most of the knowledge regarding bio-diversity in the mountains. They need to have this knowledge because it is usually the women who plant the crops, make medicines and remedies from plants and herbs, and feed their families. Crop failure can mean starvation, so, for generations, women have studied what helps plants thrive. They know how to protect the plants from pests and which varieties grow best. Women are involved at every stage, from plant-ing seeds to harvesting to food preparation.

The View from Above

Global Land Ice Measurement from Space (GLIMS) is a project that was designed to monitor the world's glaciers by observing them from space. Monitoring the glaciers provides a sensitive early indication of changes in the world brought about by global warming. At the present time, the signs are not good. All over the world, the glaciers are shrinking. Satellite images also reveal the extent of the damage done to mountain forests by extensive logging.

Knowing the range of the animals is of great importance when marking out wildlife refuge areas or monitoring the health of herds and various species of wild animals. Satellite tracking systems using the global positioning system (GPS) can actually allow researchers to keep track of single animals as each one moves in its mountain home. First, of course, the animal has to be safely captured, collared with the tracking device, and then released, unharmed, back into the wild. This task may be challenging if the animal in question is a 220-pound (100-kilogram) mountain lion! Using the tracking devices, researchers can, for example, track a herd of mountain goats to find out what their grazing patterns are.

Measuring Diversity

Biodiversity means the variety of living things. Keeping that diversity high is vital to the health of the planet. The greater a habitat's diversity, the more forms of life it supports. With diversity, life itself has more options for survival when conditions change. If a habitat is not diverse — having only one kind of vegetation, for example — a single disease can wipe out those plants — and the animals and insects that depend on that vegetation may disappear as well.

The mountains may not be seen as being as richly diverse as the rain forests or the oceans, but within the differing zones of a mountain range, such as the Rocky Moun-tains, there can be over 10,000 different species of plants and animals. The variety of small habitats within the large mountain habitat means that mountains are often richer in plants and animals than elsewhere. As we have also seen, there are plants and animals on the mountains that are found nowhere else. The most diverse region on the planet is in the tropical mountains of the Andes. Almost one fifth of the world's plant species are found there. Some of these plants may provide cures in the future for life-threatening illnesses.

What Can You Do?

What can you do to help preserve the fragile mountains and their irreplaceable treasure house of life? Here are a few ideas:

Saver Sense

One of the biggest threats to the mountain environment comes from global warming. As many people believe that this warming is a result of the build-up of carbon dioxide in the atmosphere from burning fossil fuels, one way of slowing down the effect would be to cut our consumption of these fuels. In winter, put on an extra layer of clothing instead of turning up the heat. Turn lights off when no one is in a room. Switch appliances such as televisions off properly — do not leave them on stand-by. If possible, walk or ride a bicycle to school — do not go by car. When you do need to make a longer journey, try to use public transportation or arrange rides with friends. As well as saving mountain wildlife, all these things could save your family money, which would provide a double benefit.

Sustainable Products

When you go shopping, think about who is supplying what you buy and where it comes from. Coffee, for example, is grown in highland regions in various parts of the world, such as those in Brazil, Kenya, and Papua, New Guinea. Look on the label for signs that the coffee your family buys is sold as a "fair trade" product. This means that the farmers who grew it will get a decent price for their crop. When buying wood products, ask your family to look for signs that the forest where the wood came from is properly managed.

Mountain Vacations

If you're lucky enough to take a vacation trip to one of the world's mountain areas, perhaps as a skier or a hiker, take care and keep your impact on the environment to a minimum. Do not cut wood from mountain forests to start campfires. Keep to the trails. It might be fun to go where seemingly no one has gone before, but think about the mountain plants you might be trampling underfoot. Snowmobiles might look like fun in winter, but they are noisy and polluting, disturbing the wildlife and damaging the environment. Do not leave litter in wild places. Take it home with you and, if possible, pick up any that you see.

The Write Thing to Do!

There are mountains all over the world. Wherever you live, the chances are that there will be mountains somewhere not too far away. Find out who is in charge of conservation issues in your country and find out about organizations that help protect the environment. Write to them and find out what they are doing to help protect mountains. Ask what you can do to help, too.

Web Sites

Here are a few Web sites for mountain fans to explore:

www.igf.fuw.edu.pl/hill/
Find a fairly comprehensive listing of mountain and mountain-related Web sites from around the world.

www.mountain.org
Get to know an organization dedicated to the preservation of mountain environments and cultures around the world.

www.mountainpartnership.org
This is the official Web site of the 2002 Year of the Mountain. The Mountain Partnership is a voluntary alliance of partners dedicated to improving the lives of mountain people and protecting mountain environments around the world.

www.mountainvoices.org
Read interviews with hundreds of people from mountain regions all over the world and learn about their lives.

www.peakbagger.com/cont/ worldmap.htm
Start from a map of the world showing the major mountain ranges, and begin an exploration of the world's mountains. This site includes mountain climbers' descriptions of their climbs.

www.peopleandplanet.net
Explore a large, fascinating source of information on humans and the planet they live on, including mountains and mountain people.

Glossary

acclimatization
the process of getting used to, or acclimatized to, the conditions in a particular area

algae
plant-like organisms that make their own food by converting sunlight to nutrients

alpine
describing high mountain regions generally, or specifically referring to the Alps mountains in Europe

biodiversity
the range, or variety, of living things found in an ecological system. The more diverse the living things in a habitat are, the more life within that habitat is able to survive disease and adapt to changes, such as climate variations or pest invasions.

biome
a very large habitat where living conditions are ecologically connected and broadly similar across a wide area, such as the ocean biome or the desert biome

cloud forests
forests, usually covered in clouds for much of each day, growing on tropical mountain-sides above rain forests at heights of 3300 feet (1000 m) or more; also called elfinwoods, as the trees here are smaller than true rain forest trees

dew claws
small inner claws found on the legs of some animals, usually as undeveloped toes or claws that serve little purpose

ecosystem
all of the living things in a particular place, together with the physical conditions there — such as soil composition and weather — and the ways in which all these things, both living and non-living, interact with each other

environment
a physical habitat, such as a mountain range, together with all the living things that make their home there

erosion
the wearing away of a surface by physical or chemical action, such as wind on soil

extinction
the permanent loss of a type or species of living thing from Earth when the last member of that species has died

glacier
a slow-moving river of ice formed by layers of snow piling up over many years in mountains and polar regions

global warming
the trend of the overall temperature of Earth to gradually increase. Many scientists believe that current global warming is caused by pollution that creates the green-house effect, which happens when increased levels of carbon dioxide and other chemicals in the atmosphere trap heat rising from Earth's surface, warming the globe

GPS
an acronym for "global positioning system." Widely used by explorers, scientists, and the

military, GPS trackers use signals from a network of satellites to determine an object's position anywhere on Earth

gullies
steep-sided, narrow ravines cut by water into the sides of mountains

habitat
the place where a living thing makes its home; a habitat can be as big as a mountain range or as small as the crack in a boulder

hibernation
entering into a sleep-like state; some animals hibernate to survive harsh winter conditions until spring comes and food is more plentiful

lichen
an organism formed by a partnership between an alga and a fungus

migrate
to move from one area to another, usually in search of better living conditions

nomad
a member of a tribe of people who have no fixed home but move from place to place, usually to find new pasture for their animals

plates
large, slow-moving sections of Earth's crust; movements of the plates are thought to cause of earthquakes and the formation of mountain ranges

pollinator
something that carries pollen from one flower to another so that fertilization can take place and seeds can form; the chief pollinators are insects

rain shadow
an area in the so-called shadow of a mountain range that receives very little rainfall because moist air is blocked by the mountains

refuge
a place of shelter from trouble or danger

snow line
the height on a mountain above which temperatures are below freezing and snow does not melt all year round

tree line
the height on a mountain above which conditions are too harsh for trees to grow

tundra
the cold, treeless region to the south of the north polar regions where the ground is frozen for most or all of the year

ultraviolet radiation
high-energy radiation from the sun, invisible to human eyes, that can cause damage to living tissues

Index